The Venus Pool

Wendy Falla

The Venus Pool by Wendy Falla

First Edition

© Wendy Falla 2017

Wendy Falla has asserted her authorship
and given her permission to Dempsey & Windle
for these poems to be published here.

All rights reserved. No part of this publication may be reproduced, stored in a retrieval system or transmitted in any form or by any means without the written consent of Wendy Falla, nor otherwise circulated in any form of binding or cover other than that in which it is published and without a similar condition being imposed on a subsequent purchaser.

Published by Dempsey & Windle

15 Rosetrees
Guildford
Surrey
GU1 2HS
01483 571164
dempseyandwindle.co.uk

A CIP record for this book can be obtained from the British Library

ISBN: 978-1-907435-49-2

For Jacob and Emil

Acknowledgements

Poems in this collection have appeared in:
Vortex 2007; *Rising Tides: An Anthology of Channel Island Writing*; *A Barrel of Monkeys* Anthology (Dempsey & Windle 2016); *Poems to Keep* Anthology (Dempsey & Windle 2017) and one poem is trundling around Guernsey on a bus!

The photographs on the cover are by Frederick Phillips (1926 – 2012: the author's Uncle Fred). The one on the back was taken in 1961; the one on the front is from 1962.

Thanks are due to Geraint Jennings for his help with the Jèrriais patois in *Wild Peacocks* (page 8).

Foreword

Publication of this collection holds a bittersweet sadness for me. The people who inspired many of the poems are sadly no longer alive. I often described my father and mother as the most eccentric people I know; however, that eccentricity was the journey into dementia.

I consider myself very fortunate to have been born and raised in the Channel Islands in the 1960s, before global businesses arrived and modern glass and concrete brought parts of the islands into the materialist 21st century.

My parents were children during the Occupation of the Channel Islands in WWII. It was to have a lasting effect on their lives. There is a great deal to be learned about 'make do and mend' and the importance of valuing people and friendship over objects and possessions. We live in a throwaway society. As the internet connects us to the other side of the globe, we can lose sight of those close to us. But even now, for anyone who wants a truly unique Channel Island experience – I recommend a holiday in Sark!

I had to leave the islands to appreciate how special they are. Having spent years feeling 'trapped on the rock' I jumped at the chance to study at Winchester University as a mature student. I had never written poetry until I found myself in one of Julian Stannard's poetry modules. I owe a huge debt of gratitude to him for his positive and constructive feedback and for encouraging me to write about the Channel Islands. Thanks also to Marc Brightside who has always given honest advice, even though our style and subject matter are very different.

And to my wonderful writer's group, 'Room 1'- who know this project inside out and have given encouragement, in meetings, by email and at the end of the phone. Thank you!

Wendy Falla
2017

Contents

Resilience	1
Hiatus	2
A Letter from my Mother	4
Finches	6
The Homecoming	7
Wild Peacocks	8
Her Last Cigarette	9
Grumpa	10
Ancestry	12
Muriel and Lionel	14
Preparing for a Holiday in Sark	15
Temps Passé	16
Customer Services	18
Fat Man's Misery	20
In Search of the Perseids	21
Thrift	22
Serious Thrift	24
Also representing…	25
Harvesting	26
Recipe for Black Butter	27
Cider Making	28
Wishful Thinking	29
Who Knew?	30
Red Phenomena	31
Symmetry	32
Carnival	33
The Making of a Tradition	34
Preparation for the Battle	35
The Conger Eel Confessional	36
The Barber Shop	37
Everything's going Swimmingly!	38
Baby! We Need to Talk!	40
Conundrum	43
Eco Lyrics	44
The Cynic's Guide to Love	46
The Lost Word	47
After the Storm	48

Resilience

If you want something done,
ask a busy man.
He'll do it straight away
and to perfection, at the first attempt.
A meal or bottle of favourite spirit in return
and a willingness to respond
with a smile when he asks you
to sew on a button or hem his trousers.
Remember back to a time when they had nothing,
when the only thing to be shared was an embrace
and a sympathetic ear.
There is a great deal to be learned from
a small isolated community under pressure:
stoicism, resilience, determination
and an optimism that the dark days will surely pass.

Hiatus

5.30am the alarm sounds
I read the notes I wrote last night
I dress, let the dogs out, make tea
and relish half an hour of free time:
I'll type this poem up right now.
6.30am my teenager awakes and comes downstairs.
'Mum I can't find any socks'
'Try the airing cupboard'
'I've looked.'
I go and find an almost matching pair
and decide to clean the bathroom
by which time we need to leave for the station.
Once he's dropped off, I rush home to continue the poem,
except, stuck in traffic, a special offer at the garden centre
catches my eye – car laden with compost.
I stop for coffee and read newspapers
'Oh my God!' the mobile mechanic is due!

Back home, he's waiting and I leave him with the car
as the postman arrives - at least no bills today.
Two messages on the ansaphone, both from my mother.
She says it's nothing urgent or important,
which means it is, so I call: that passes another hour,
until the mechanic knocks on the door.
'Can you come and pump the brake pedal for me?'
Gosh, five hours since I took the dogs out,
off we go, assorted breeds and ages,
some lag behind, others are out of sight.
But this afternoon, when they are tired out,
I shall write uninterrupted.

Alone in the house I sigh with relief.
My mother phones to tell me what she forgot to say this morning.
I peg out the washing, write a shopping list, water indoor plants,
dust the piano and sit down to play for five minutes,
but two hours pass in a flash and I'm late to meet my son's train,
And of course he is starving.
'What have you done today Mum?'
'Oh, you know, this and that, tried to write a poem.'

Back home, I cook, we eat, I feed the dogs and take them
for another walk.
At 9pm I pour a glass of wine and study the words I typed this morning,
But a great deal has happened since then,
and I no longer recognise them.

A Letter From My Mother

Let me start by telling you, dear,
the tortoises are fine.
Val is hiding under the rhubarb
and Annie is burrowing into the base
of the eucalyptus tree.
Your father gets slower and
more forgetful by the day.
His appetite is good, as is his mood,
provided he has possession of the TV remote control
and the local newspaper open at the obituaries page.
The tortoise summer house has been repainted,
I'm sure they'll soon be too big to share.
With their pre-historic mouths
they are tucking in to local strawberries
and Spanish cantaloupes.
I fear your father has swallowed his teeth
which makes menu planning
rather challenging:
tinned fruit and ice cream is
our standard meal replacement.
Post hibernation
I gave the tortoises a tepid bath
and then anointed them with olive oil
(extra virgin of course)
to nourish their shells.
I can't get your father into the shower
since he slipped and had to be rescued
by the paramedics and fire brigade.
The bath has become a kind of storage receptacle
I wash his feet in a plastic bowl.
One wonders where it will all end
when the tortoises are on the rampage.
I've barricaded the salad plants with
an armadillo of corrugated iron
and they've completely obliterated the arum lilies.

Pills, pills, pills and more pills -
your father is quite the one man band
his stomach rattles like a maracca
punctuated by the thud of his two
walking sticks on the floorboards.

If the tortoises continue to eat
as if fruit is going out of fashion,
by autumn we may need a second
hibernation box unless we stack
one on top of the other like torty bunk beds.
I thought it was a good idea to
place a little brass bell
on the coffee table beside your father
and the only way I can cope with that
decision is by turning off my hearing aids.
I've discovered the problem re
the missed calls you keep finding
on your mobile and landline
your father can no longer tell the difference
between our phone handset and TV remote control.
Last night he flushed his pyjama bottoms
down the loo, flooding the bathroom,
which leaked through the ceiling into
the sitting room, right above the television
where Croatia were playing Portugal
in the European cup. Water seeped inside
the set, causing a dark shadow across the screen,
no wonder Croatia missed their penalty shot,
the goal post was blurred and distorted.
But life goes on my dear …

Finches

Quite by chance I saw you
sitting calmly and serene
within the shade of the vine clad pergola:
you were staring into the distance
observing bees plunging funnel flowered
hollyhocks, foxgloves and majestic arum lilies
while finches gorged on nettle seeds,
their puffed chested bodies causing
the stems to sway.
Or were you staring into the portals of time
beyond our current generations,
back to where we came from
and where we might go to in the future,
migrants of the middle ages,
resourceful survivors,
growers, makers, builders,
can turn our hands to anything.
And at your funeral,
so many said how helpful you had been,
and caring, be it family or friends
or a stranger in need,
as we had once been strangers in need.
A woodpecker flew into the scene,
startling me and scattering the finches,
staking his claim on the bird feeder.
As silently as you had appeared
you slipped away
but I expect to see you again soon
in your beloved garden.

The Homecoming

I sailed in on the Nonpareil, my arms outstretched like wings,
and threw my bag onto a horse drawn cart – no label required.
I stepping-stoned my way across the bay on boulders slick and wet,
stopping to pop bladder vraic between finger and thumb,
delighting in its viscosity.
I laid your name out in brown sea belts and sugar kelp
decorated with paisley swirls of china fragments
and small curved shells,
like new born baby's toes, sand dusted and salt encrusted.
Lunch was foraged razor clams fried in a skillet over an open fire,
with a knob of my Mother's hand-churned butter.

I toasted you with Malbec from a tin mug, reflecting on temps passé.
At your home, the door ajar for the bantams to run in and out,
as if you had just gone to Chapel, or the post office.
The aroma of Lux flakes lingered around the twin tub,
and your Coal Tar soap still wet on the wooden draining board.
A pig's head soaking in a bucket of water with garlic and herbs,
brawn in the making: you didn't expect to leave us.
Beside the telephone, a bowl of bottle tops for guide dogs for the blind,
four knitting needles working their way around the heel of a sock,
a shrivelled apple core and a half written letter to Wendy.

Wild Peacocks

At Jaspellerie, my childhood home, the peacocks strut.
At dusk they roost on low apple boughs,
their magnificent tales draping down like silken scarves.
The path to the front door is edged with Calendula and Marigolds.
Tin roofed house with Rayburn kitchen,
heat or hot water, you can't have both.
Rain collected in water butts, boiled before drinking.
'STINK or SWIM' says the sign in the bathroom
above a basket of swimsuits to fit all sizes.
Raincoats and Wellingtons to fit all too…
'There's no such thing as bad weather,' Says Grumpa,
'only inappropriate attire.'
Himself a man for all seasons, a man for all reasons,
pop-pops as he sucks on his pipe,
clothes perforated by cinder burns.
It seems only yesterday *j'pâlêmes du Jèrriais*
dans la tchuîsinne jusqu'ès p'tits crapauds,
tchi qui avait mouothi la s'maine dé d'vant,
et tchi qui s'n allait êt' né la s'maine d'auprès
while drinking smoky tea with milk straight from the cow,
pustules of cream rising to the surface,
Calvados chasers and crumbly sultana Madelaines,
all lost to the passing of time.

Her Last Cigarette

And so it was, the day after her
ten hour honeymoon,
Muriel awoke alone
in the eaves of her father's house.
She pulled on her clothes and
slipped off her wedding ring
leaving it in the ashtray
on the bedside table of polished walnut.
She went to work in the fields
as her new husband sailed on the tide.
God rays striped the room
with dust particles and talcum powder,
vapours of eau de Cologne,
lavender and Du Maurier.

On the eve of her eightieth birthday,
she smoked her last cigarette
and slowly climbed the ladder to the loft.
She slipped off her wedding ring,
leaving it in the ashtray
on the bedside table edged with cigarette burns.
Slipping between the sheets
of unfulfilled dreams and faded memories,
she took her final breath
and exhaled into the dust particles
which escaped through the skylight
and into the night air.

Grumpa

Take another look – beyond the withering shell.
Here is a man who's never told a lie or been in debt.
A man who held down seven jobs to raise his family
and still found time to volunteer.
He would give you the coat off his back,
a little threadbare and with a few dog hairs attached,
but he would give it willingly and not expect anything in return.

He could set sail in the small boat he built with his father,
catch a fish on a homemade hook,
gut it with a knife he'd sharpened on a whetstone
and cook it over a fire lit with two sticks or a flint.
Here is a man who's known sorrow: his wife died young,
but he gave thanks for the time they had together,
raised his young family alone and then learned to love again.

This old man looks longingly at fillet steak in the village shop
remarking that it's far beyond his modest means,
but on leaving, stuffs ten pound notes
into British Red Cross and Cancer Research collecting boxes.
Here is a man who has never held a driving licence
but can saddle a horse, ride bare back or
drive a carriage and four across La Coupée in a storm.

His bear paw hands can milk a nervous goat
and then make cheeses …
rolling the marshmallow curds in fine herbs
he has grown from seed.
He flouts convention: smokes, drinks and eats whatever he likes.
His wedding suit still fits him, worn to Chapel on Sundays,
a snazzy double breasted pin striped number
any Mafioso grandee would be proud of.

Now, as he dozes in a chair in the corner of the restaurant,
unshaven, he's growing a full set of whiskers for 'Movember',
an acquaintance approaches and shakes his hand,
'Are you free for lunch on Sunday, Jacques?'
'Sorry, no, I'm a centenarian now,' he says, adding,
'oh, go on then, yes!'
He whispers to me, 'I should so hate to disappoint them.'
I smile to myself ... there will be no chance of that!

Ancestry

The stranger invited me in.
Had I known whose hand I shook,
I would have curtseyed low and blushed.
'You have the look,' he said.
Each step I take is a link to a century past.
He empties my ancestors from a cardboard tube,
un-scrolling and smoothing them over his table,
weighing down handfuls of cousins with heavy books.
He unfolds my letter, pointing with a baton
to the names I have mentioned.
Nine centuries ago my forefathers
sailed into St Peter Port,
mistaking it for England.
Fast-forward three hundred years:
familiar names appear to me,
unfurling like leaves in spring.
Theadora-Dorothea, Jehanne, Rozelle, the female line.
Grandmère's voice echoes in my head,
pointing to a Vermeer-style portrait,
eyebrows knitted in a frown:
'that teenage floozy eloped with a Dutchman.'
Melanie Rosalie married Emil de Groot and thereafter vanished.
In tiny spider writing,
Great Grand-ma's thirteen daughters vie for space,
gathering now around this table,
grey and gauzy Miss Havershams,
stitching quilts and knitting socks,
while weeping, hearts broken.
My grandmother, one of them,
mourning her twin brothers,
precious boys lost at Ypres.
Guido Le Strange appeared in the Middle Ages,
a knight, a dueller, a Casanova
and here he is, beside me.
It feels like popping candy in my blood.
Air ... breathe, breathe ... count to ten.

John Stranger has less èlan than Guido le Strange,
but the sparkle in his eyes and the way
he kisses my cheek transcends the generations.
'Are you feeling warm my dear ?
allow me to assist with your jacket.'
Over his shoulder, the great aunts slither beneath the table,
Grandmère winks and waggles her finger;
Melanie Rosalie gives me a shy smile and a knowing look
before vanishing with a swish of her skirt.

Muriel and Lionel

Muriel caresses the barnacled hand,
the tremor subsides.
'Do you remember summers long ago?
When skies were always cloudless blue.
We'd freewheel down the harbour hill,
glide into the water at dusk
and swim to your little boat.
There we'd be gently rocked by the lapping waves,
or the movement of an undulating swell.
On moonless nights we lay naked,
gazing at the stars,
waking to the lilac sky before dawn,
plunging into the water and hurrying home.
Do you remember prawning in gullies?
and setting out spinners for mackerel?
Oh! and what about caving ...
the dripping crystalline ceilings and
walls studded with sea anemones
the size of small fisted rubies.
Harvest festivals and cider-making,
bonfires and barn dances,
songs sung in the old language
with accordion accompaniment.
The cradle you crafted as a little boat
on crescent moon rockers,
never held a child.
The christening gown I stitched
has been folded in tissue for fifty years.
Half a century ... Do you remember, dear?'

Lionel shakes his head,
'I'm sorry lass, you look familiar,
were you once perhaps a friend of my sister? '

Preparing for a holiday in Sark

'Any advice on what to bring?'
I ask the host of the B & B,
'Waterproofs, wellington boots,
a torch and a bathing suit.'
The latter was already packed,
The former, I decided to contemplate.

Having made many friends.
'Is there anything I can bring?'
could result in requests for
antibiotics for a cow,
canvas for cross stitch
Kombucha tea or Harissa paste.

Small car-less island,
a step back in time.
The locals so friendly and helpful.
Perfect destination, even on rainy days.
Walks, boat trips, rambling, caving,
Concerts, coasteering, oh! and a chocolate factory!

Temps Passé

Centuries ago
farmers and fishermen
left their bean crock in
the embers of the oven,
to return to a hearty meal
at the end of the day.

Dried beans, hung from the rafters,
shaken from their papery husks,
soaked overnight and placed in a large pot
with onions, garlic, a pigs trotter or beef,
covered in water or stock and cooked
overnight or throughout the day.
Cabbage Loaf accompaniment,
crusty bread baked between brassica leaves,
to prevent burning should the baker be distracted,
thickly spread with mother's home churned butter.

Five hundred years ago,
farmers planted crops in the spring,
prayed in the Fishermans' Chapel
and set sail across the Atlantic.
Currents took them to Nova Scotia,
Newfoundland and the Gaspé Peninsula.
They created an industry far from home.
Fishermen, crew, coopers and gutters,
the dryers and the salters,
clerks and general storemen.
Names taken across the Atlantic
in the sixteenth century
Endure to this day.

Salt cod, precious cargo
in barrels in the hold,
transported to the good Catholics
of the Indies and Europe,
to be sold or bartered
for tea and silks, cotton and spices.
Men in a race against tides and trade winds,
to return to their beloved Channel Islands
across the Atlantic,
in time for the harvest.

Customer Services

Sent: 16th May 2014 09.39 BST
Subject: General Enquiry
From: alanandbettythetourists@hereandthere.com
To: infoattheholidayoffice@tinycarlessisland.com

Dear Sir/Madam

Last year, my wife and I spent a very pleasant week on your island. Every day we met an elderly lady who pushed her bicycle along instead of riding it. I recall she wore a floppy sun hat. We had some lovely chats. Unfortunately, we've lost the scrap of paper with her name and address. Have you any idea who she is? We are returning this year and would love to renew the acquaintance.

Alan and Betty Tourist

*

Sent: 16th May 2014 16.44 BST
Subject: Reply to yours
From: infoattheholidayoffice@tinycarlessisland.com
To: alanandbettythetourists@hereandthere.com

Dear Alan and Betty

Thank you for your email. Do you realise you've described 50% of the population of the island?

Sincerely yours
Zeta in the holiday office.

*

Sent: 17th May 2014 08.51 BST
Subject: Reply to your reply
From: alanandbettythetourists@hereandthere.com
To: infoattheholidayoffice@tinycarlessisland.com

Dear Zeta

Thank you for your prompt reply. What a shame you can't help us, having chatted about wine, we were planning to bring her a bottle of our favourite red.

Kind regards
Alan and Betty Tourist

Sent: 17th May 2014 12.16BST
Subject: Eureka!
From: alanandbettythetourists@hereandthere.com
To: infoattheholidayoffice@tinycarlessisland.com

Dear Alan and Betty

Ah-ha! You mean Gabrielle Lajoie! Take the road towards La Coupée and look out for the tin roofed house with pale blue picket fence and the garden full of gnomes on the right hand side.

Zeta.

Fat Man's Misery

'This can't be the way,' I said to my friend, as we peeked over the edge of the cliff. And yet, we were with a recommended local guide. Before we set off he looked me up and down. I must confess I was not exactly slender then, but a little less rounded than now. Did he wonder if the rope would bear my weight? It did!

Over the edge of the headland we went, slipping into a crevice like a lazy eyelid in the rock. Crawl and drop, crawl and drop through tunnels and chimneys, the sound of water, tidal, dripping, tumbling, and the smell of the sea. A turquoise light tinged with gold refracted into the cave. It made judgement deceptive; the stepping-stone just below the surface left me thigh-deep in water.

Stalactites appeared to be within reach but were elusively a stretch too far. Stripes on stones came alive when wet. Long strands of seaweed snaked in the shadows. Day-dreaming in this subterranean world, I was brought to my senses as the sea breached the mouth of the cave with a gush: rushing in, almost sweeping me off my feet.

The guide beckoned, in panic we followed.

I feared we would drown, but there, at the back of the cave, was a narrow crevasse. A 'Fat Man's Misery!' Would I fit through it? Breathing in, to make me thin, that you are reading this poem proves … I did!

In Search of The Perseids

Dark, darkest, darkness,
blindly into the night we go,
abandoning our clothes
along with our inhibitions.
Bare feet engulfed by sharp wet shingle,
staggering like drunkards to the water's edge.
The beach slopes steeply
and deeply into the water we glide,
anaesthetised by the cold
but exhilarated and smiling for no reason.

Far, further, faraway
from the shore we swim,
in search of The Perseids,
eyes focused on the billion and more stars above us,
oblivious to the underlying currents,
watching, waiting, searching for a movement,
a flash, a streak, a tail of fire bright, white light …
Then on the horizon a blood orange orb
emerges from the sea and ascends turning golden.

We gasp at the spectacle,
and when your hand reaches
out to me beneath the surface,
capturing for eternity a meteor's reflection
within a cloud of bubbles,
my eyes are fixed on the sky above,
and when I turn,
you have gone …

Thrift

Mother's everlasting chicken,
roast on Sunday,
cold cuts with salad on Monday,
casseroled remains on Tuesday,
curried tiny chicken shreds on Wednesday,
bones boiled for soup on Thursday,
just in time for conger eel steaks on Friday.
Don't pull that face ...
baked in the Aga, dotted with butter, drizzled with cream
sprinkled with marigold petals (optional) when in season.

Auntie's infinity wool creations
seamless miracles
knitted on circular needles,
a pullover for her husband,
cabled with ropes and anchors,
leather patched elbows,
blanket stitched hems,
unravelled to make school jumpers,
remnants crocheted into Red Cross blankets,
pom-poms for woolly hats and scraps for the cat to play with.

Grumpa's self-renewing garden,
open trench composting,
none of your modern rotating plastic bin lark,
dig a spit and chuck your peelings in,
cover with soil and repeat,
keep back a handful of beans to sow next season,
tomato seeds too, why buy them? Waste of packaging.
Pay postage? You're nuts! You must have money to burn ...
take a cutting, divide a root,
give sunflowers as a gift.

Water, water everywhere, surrounded by the stuff
a moody brine which ebbs and flows.
Have a bath? You must be joking!
A whole month's drinking water down the plughole.
We mustn't waste it …
Here! Wash in this bowl then empty it on the beans,
do the dishes in the sink and use the water on the rhubarb,
soap suds keep aphids at bay.
A machine to wash clothes? Whatever next?
Organic? You don't know the meaning of the word!

Serious Thrift

Hedge-gathered wild garlic,
blackberries on a hot afternoon,
sloes ready for pricking and drowning in gin,
green filberts, picked before squirrels squirrel them away,
ripened in a box in the airing cupboard.
Medlars, forget the jokes about their appearance
as prized as truffles, bletted, and no pigs required in the search.

To the beach we go, with a net and some buckets,
a bag of coarse salt and a sharp penknife.
Whelks – fishy chewing gum, winkles and clams.
Razor fish magic as they rise vertically from the sand.
A host of prawns, a scattering of limpets,
samphire and dulce, dandelion leaves.
We spent a couple of summer afternoons
foraging with the children
but - dear God! My parents, as children,
spent five years doing this,
every day, rain or shine.

Tante Marianne tied fine nets between trees
to capture song birds,
sixty roasted in a tray,
meat eaten, bones boiled for gruel.
It is how they survived the Occupation –
all those years ago.

Also Representing …

The antipodean contingent
cry crocodile tears into thimbles of sherry
and snowballs of advocaat
'a very English thing to do
at wakes' said cousin Grace,
'It was terrible shock!'
'He was such a strong man …'

It's been sixteen years
since they returned to
the island of their birth.
They mouth the hymns,
keep eyes open through prayers
and yawn through the committal.
They are also representing spouses,
children, grandchildren and their partners
who meant nothing at all to my father
who latterly lived in the moment
gauging time by each pill or nursing home meal
and could communicate only
by squeezing my hand.

Harvesting

You would not believe it!
My mother systematically
scours the tables at jumble sales,
buying things I know aren't her size.
At home, the harvesting begins.

Starting with the buttons:
if not used for a garment of her own,
they are neatly stitched
to small pieces of card,
and sold at charity sales.

She has an eye for design and pattern.
A blouse or a dress which has gone out of fashion
can be reborn with contrast
collar, cuffs, hem or pockets.
'Nothing is wasted' is her mantra.

Attractive old plates for edible gifts.
Vintage saucers when giving a plant.
Dainty tea cups for candles and pin cushions.
Any decorative containers for planting herbs,
often with a hand written recipe attached.

Tiny scraps of fabric for patchwork,
dolls clothes, rag rugs, covered buttons.
It pains her to see things heading for the bin.
fragments too small, damaged or moth eaten,
well … they make the best fire lighters of all!

Recipe for Black Butter

Light your fire in the afternoon
so the men can add logs in the evening
and all through the night.

Industrious women, heads bent
over vast urns, peel 700lb of apples.
They sing folk songs in the old language,
accompanied by fiddle and accordion.

Take ten gallons or so of freshly made cider,
the cloudy dregs from the crusher are fine.
Simmer in the Bachin until reduced by half
and forming an amber jelly,
this may take two nights and a day.
Then add the chopped apples, two buckets at a time ...

Stir in twenty-five pounds of sugar,
twenty lemons finely chopped,
three fat sticks of well crushed liquorice root
and three pounds of all-spice, finely ground
in the alabaster mortar.

Simmer to a smooth puree, constantly stirring.
Leave to cool slightly before decanting into jars.
Bon appetit!

Cider Making

Leaves become flame flecked and
night scented stock perfumes the air.
In the cobwebbed half-light of the cider barn
a well-tempered mare pulls a stone wheel
around a granite crusher filled to the brim
with autumn's tawny harvest.
The mash is hessian wrapped,
placed into clamps and pressed.
While the liquor is extracted,
collected, casked or bottled,
the nocturnal watchers tell ghost stories.
Owl calls give way to a nightingale's song,
its last before migration,
the promise of the new day
is a faint blush on the horizon.
Let's raise a toast to the year's first pressing of cider.

Wishful Thinking

It saddens me to leave you
We both know I can't stay
I had hoped to take you with me …
For a weekend, maybe a few days.
Your room's been ready for a long time now.
North facing, it overlooks the garden
and beyond that a stream,
a meadow full of cows
dilapidated barns,
a haven for wildlife,
a roost for owls,
a rookery centuries old.
Wild birds cluster around the feeder,
squirrels leap from tree to tree
driving the dogs mad, teasing them.
You would love it.

You can bring anything you like,
to make it feel like home …
maybe not the Art Deco dining suite
with sideboard the size of a tank,
and perhaps not the post-war utility wardrobes
with their stripy fake veneer.
But your favorite chair, and your Louis Seize bed.
'Your' room has a fireplace and a mantelpiece.
I could look after you, bring you Camp coffee in china cup
with a silver spoon, even though you don't take sugar.
With a slice of home-made cake or still-warm scones.
Put your feet up, get your knitting out,
doze off and no one will mind.
Have the TV too loud – there are no neighbours to disturb.
Go into the garden in your dressing gown and slippers,
or stark naked if that's what your heart desires.
Gaze at the moon and the stunning sunrises and sunsets.
At the close of day I will read to you until you fall asleep
and all will be at peace in our world.

Who Knew?

Who knew? who cared?
and of those of us who cared,
who knew how dire the consequences?
of a life well lived,
frugally,
thoughtfully,
compassionately,
but with humour
and a zest for life,
with a song in her heart,
a sparkle in her eyes,
and a cigarette in her hand
or bouncing on her lower lip,
or scorching the edge of the dining table,
or the prayer book ledge in Chapel
and the walnut dashboard
of Gumpa's most prized Delahaye Coupé.
What exuberance, what fun,
what a nonchalant existence,
a slash of crimson lipstick,
a laugh louder than any other,
without a care in the world, no debts, nor regrets
who knew, who really knew, the real you ?

Red Phenomena

For a month, every day after rainfall,
we sat above Derrible Bay.
We needed a certain kind of sunset
and a slight breeze, preferably from the east.
After an hour, we were poised to walk away
but the dog stayed motionless,
his eyes fixed on some distant speck.
The breeze picked up and ruffled the surfaces of the puddles.
Then colour came into the sky,
pinks, purples, peaches, shades of orange
and red, red sinking low, towards the horizon,
painting the sky with flames,
creating a path of fire
and validating my memory of how it was before ...

Symmetry

My perfect child
of twenty-seven summers,
today
I collected your ashes.
In melancholic symmetry
they weigh exactly
the same as you did
as a newborn.

Carnival

Church doors close at dusk.
Canticles fade to murmurs,
incense lingers in the air.
Fake-jewelled women arm in arm
with gurning fools step out into the night.
Silks shimmer, velvets fold,
and draped in feathers, fur and finery
they discard their inhibitions.
Casting off age and infirmity they walk beside
cross-dressing youths and androgynous muses.
Anything goes and nobody knows
who's behind the mask or makeup.
Wigs, turbans, top hats, tiaras,
veils and fedoras.
A world of dreams and make-believe.
Sleep-deprived but energised by moonlight,
thriving on adrenalin,
absinthe and eau de vie,
revellers dance in the streets and alleyways.
Tall stilt-walkers cast shadows
over swan necked Nubians.
Princes, paupers and snake-oil talkers
forget their positions or earning a living.
Tonight they mingle as one,
moving to the beat of the carnival drum.

The Making of a Tradition

A celebration parade in honour of the 1902 Coronation of Edward VII and Queen Alexandra proved so popular that the organisers decided to repeat it the following year. It was to become an annual event. At the turn of the twentieth century, carriages decorated with floral garlands were drawn by horses were cheered on by locals and visitors. The origin of the 'Battle' came about as flowers were ripped from carriages and thrown into the crowd, in anticipation that they would be thrown back. The Battle of Flowers stopped during The Great War, and again during WWII, when the Channel Islands were the only part of the British Isles to be occupied by enemy forces. Once re-instated, and with the islands becoming a popular holiday destination, the Battle of Flowers grew year by year. Horses were replaced by motorised floats. As soon as one year's battle was over, planning would start for the next: shrouded in secrecy, as the entrants competed for trophies and awards.

The battle is very much a community event. The largest floats are entered by Parishes and the smaller ones by clubs, associations and families. As fresh flower heads are used – flown in especially from the UK and Holland - they need to be attached to the framework at the last minute. Teams of volunteers often work into the early hours to get their float completed and ready to head to the arena. Many of the same volunteers then take part in the parade, dressing up in the theme of their float and either being a fixture of it, or walking alongside. The Battle has grown from modest origins to the highlight of Jersey's year. In the past there have been paper petals dropped from aircraft, fireworks, and now a Moonlight Parade. In addition, the fun fair comes to the island for a two week period. A truly spectacular family event for locals and visitors alike.

Preparation for the Battle

Exhausted, always,
it's part of the fun.
Volunteers open box upon box
of fragrant chrysanthemums
laying them out across the barn,
sorted by colour.

Designers, makers,
costumiers, face-painters,
choreographers, musicians,
the community
coming together,
across generations.

Everyone works through the night
attaching flower heads
to handmade structures,
and despite lack of sleep
they dress up, put on a smile
and join in with the cavalcade.

The lure of a good day out
for locals and holidaymakers
from nought to ninety-nine
something for everyone.
And of course
it NEVER rains on Battle of Flowers Day

The Conger Eel Confessional

Can I tell you about the Conger?
I need to get it off my chest,
a childhood so blighted by the bloody things
that it's followed me into adulthood.
It's like this: my father cuts a fisherman's
hair for free and in return, he calls around
on a Friday with a live conger eel
in a bucket. Every Friday!
By means of the eels' restriction,
the bucket will jump around the back yard
until my father, who's probably been trying to listen to the radio,
will say 'right, let's put him out of his misery,'
and takes the bucket and the coal shovel out behind the shed.
Whack, whack, whack! – at which point I'm likely to disappear.
As a child I'd practise my scales VERY LOUDLY
Or put 45's on the turn table at FULL VOLUME.
And the next time I see Mr Conger,
he, or a tranche of him, will be relaxing in a stoneware fish kettle,
half steeped in milk with a scattering of chopped onion for company.
Seasoned with salt and pepper, the lid goes on to his coffin
and into the Aga for the best part of the afternoon.
An hour before serving, when the milk has turned into
something resembling cottage cheese,
the eel will be dotted with butter
and sprinkled with marigold petals (optional, in season).
The result is skin as tough as old leather,
which, when pierced with the point of a knife,
oozes fleshy juices the colour and consistency
of wallpaper paste.
And so this is why, if we're due to arrive on a Friday tea time,
we tell my mother we have eaten.
Even if we haven't.
We once told her we had become vegetarians,
and for a whole week she served us beetroot
and bread and butter for every meal.
Except on Sunday when she made a trifle.

The Barber Shop

When I was young my Grumpa owned a barber shop.
Open from early morning when he cleaned the windows,
until evening when he lit the barber's pole.
Chairs of chrome and creaking leather,
green and black Art Deco relics,
spun on their bases
from mirror to basin and back again.
Businessmen on their way to town offices
called in for cut-throat razor shaves.
I can hear the slap of the blade on the strop
the hiss of the steriliser,
snip-snip of the scissors,
the buzz of the clippers.
Feel the heat from the cabinet of hot towels.
All manner of embrocation and friction rubs
pungent, exotic, shampoos and aftershaves
in regimented bottles above the wooden till.
Soap, leather and cigar smoke.
Iodine massaged into scalps for baldness,
Styptic pencils for shaving nicks.
I swept up the hair with a child sized dustpan and brush,
and rubber stamped the paper bags
for cigarettes, matches and
'something for the weekend sir?'
This modest temple to hirsuteness,
vibrant with gossip and intrigue,
where a politician waited next to a fisherman,
a viscount passed the time of day with a window cleaner,
an occasional priest, or a prisoner handcuffed to his jailor.
'short back and sides sir?'
Fathers bringing sons for their first haircut.
'It will all end in tears and a wonky fringe
if you don't sit still, sonny Jim!'
Grumpa standing all day, never complaining.
Ten minutes for a light-up-and-inhale lunch
and tea from his thermos.
'Keep the change Sir? Thank you kindly.'
All gone now, all gone

Everything's going just swimmingly!

Look at the state of this kitchen! he said,
when did you last mop the floor or empty the bin?
What are you doing sitting here all day?
call yourself a writer?
J K Rowling churns out books at the drop of a hat!
'Harry Potter isn't poetry dear.'
Is there anything to eat? Why haven't you done the shopping?
We boys can't survive on coffee and dog hugging like you do …

He's right of course, I've been here a while,
but in between sitting I've weeded the veg patch
and mowed the lawn.
I've taken the dogs out too many times to count
and groomed them and trimmed their claws.
I've ironed for hours and baked a cake.
I admit, I've put on weight, the dreaded meno-unmentionable,
but that's not the reason my thighs now meet in the middle,
the dimpled flesh isn't cellulite …

And so I took my notebook down to the sand bank
and lay on my front at the waterline making notes.
Turning over, I closed my eyes for a moment,
and that's where he found me.
'This writing lark isn't earning us a living,' he said,
'it doesn't put bread on the table or beer in the fridge,
when did you last clean the bathroom and water the plants?
And we've run out of cheese … again!'
I have to admit it fell on deaf ears,
I was thinking about a new character
based on someone I knew a few years ago,
an elective mute with whom I've lost touch.

I'd been here so long that my thighs had fused,
the dimpled flesh wasn't dimples at all, but scales.
The pen slipped from my hand as the skin
between my fingers webbed.
I peered to where my toes had been: my tail twitched.

The tide came in with a rapidity that only happens here on the reef.
My last glance at the complaining man
was as I briefly looked back to my new
Monsoon sandals abandoned on the sand.
How thrilled I had been to buy them in the sale,
sadly, no use to me now

Baby! We Need to Talk!

It's starting earlier than ever: not talking.
I largely blame the mothers,
although not exclusively so,
for not talking to their children
and often not to their partners either.
Today's twenty-first century babies are strapped
into forward facing designer buggies
while their mothers push them along
listening to their IPods through headphones,
and chatting or texting on mobile phones.

Toddlers are being trundled around supermarkets
strapped into trolleys
while their mothers continue to listen to their IPods
and talk on their mobile phones rather than
talking to their offspring about the colour of the vegetables,
how much they weigh and the cost,
or what's in season,
different shapes of fruit
and what they require to make a meal.

There are the children who never shop for food:
they are alienated from shop staff and the rest of humankind.
Their weary parents buy online,
because they work all day.
Groceries are delivered in the evening,
once the children have gone to bed.
They have no idea where it comes from!
No idea of the cost or how the seemingly never ending supply
of consumables are produced.

Children of all ages are slouched on sofas
or lying across the nation's sitting room floors
watching television while their just-home-from work
frazzled parent is microwaving a ready meal
and checking his or her emails.

As technology progresses
and the choice of television channels grow,
so the life experiences of our children diminishes.
Gone forever is the adventure in the woods,
cooking on a campfire, beach-combing,
asking questions all the time
AND getting a response from their parents.
To-day's youngsters live their lives through
Facebook, Twitter, SnapChat and Instagram.
They drive around the track of Super Mario
and the only 'action' they have is within the creative narrative
of graphically violent console games.
They become dependent on their online friends
Who can be anywhere in the world, in any time zone.
They post online updates to these cyber ghosts
and move on to the next level of the game.

I can't claim to be the perfect parent,
nor anywhere near approaching it,
but less than a generation ago
my children sat in a pram facing me,
we talked, recited nursery rhymes, sang songs,
met people along the way and counted cars and buses.
We knew our neighbours and
sometimes spoke to strangers with dogs.
We laughed in the rain and walked for miles.

I used my mobile phone if I had to make an urgent call
not if I felt like telling a friend I'd just seen a fantastic outfit,
or if I couldn't find what I wanted in a supermarket.
I didn't phone my husband, parents, distant cousins
or old school friends to ask what I should buy instead ...
I used my initiative and purchased the best alternative.

A friend recently commented
that he'd read an article saying
that the shape of children today is changing.
They spend so much time on the sofa
sitting with lap tops on their knees
that they are losing their hips!
Ah! So, this is the cause of a generation of boys
who can't keep their jeans up ...
creating the trend to show an expense of designer underpants.
I shall ponder that conundrum for my next rant!

Conundrum

You are the ghost light
arced across the sky
long after the meteor's tail
fades from the naked eye

You are the memory of scent
embedded into the fabric
of a scarf you wore six months ago
discovered today in a drawer

You are on the tip of my tongue
that can't quite be discerned exotic ingredient
so difficult to source a recipe
which slips away before I can name it

Were you the one? or could have been him?
If only I'd had the patience
to overlook imperfection
before I realised what love was …

Eco Lyrics

When the last bee has died
And the final bird has flown,
When your house has turned to dust
And you're sitting all alone
In those rags you call your clothes
You're so tired that you can't sleep
So dehydrated you can't weep,
Will you begin to wonder why?

It's too late to save the world
The planet's dying and you knew it
So many chances but you blew it
It's too late to save the world.

You used to book your holidays
Park up your car and fly away
And each year you went a little further
And each year it cost you more.
Don't you worry or regret it
Put the whole damned lot on credit
You think that you deserve it
And you keep coming back for more.

It's too late to save the world
The planet's dying and you knew it
So many chances but you blew it
It's too late to save the world

I'm not asking you
To give up everything,
Just be mindful in your choices.
Don't keep taking if you've got nothing to bring.
Can't you hear the starving children's voices?
See the casualties of war?
And all the misplaced refugees:
Do they even know what the fighting's for?

Is it too late to save the world?
The planet's dying and we know it.
Our children's future, don't ignore it!
Do your share to save the world.

The Cynic's Guide to Love

*L*ies: the beginning of the end. Big ones, small ones, white and slightly grey ones, whoppers, heart stoppers, convoluted tales of extraordinary deviousness.

*O*ver it: Over him, overall a disastrous experience ... Never to be forgotten or repeated ... Until the next time.

*S*tab: the quickest way to a man's heart, straight through his chest wall with a six inch knife, blade, ice pick or any other suitably sharp implement.

*T*rust: no longer exists in this relationship, flew out of the window hand in hand with truth, never to return.

*L*eaving: packing bags and moving on. Discarding all those significant little gifts, notes attached to the fridge door and the half eaten chocolate cake.

*O*ther: significant or not, him, her, another man, another woman ... another time, another place, universe, dimension ... maybe.

*V*alentine: Ha Ha Ha, I laughed so much I nearly wet myself! You opened the door naked, with a wry smile and a huge erection ... Or was it the other way around?

*E*motions: Mixed, running wild, out of control, red-raw to the point of bleeding, open wounds, feelings too near the surface.
EXHAUSTED !

The Lost Word

Two vowels, two consonants,
small, compact, only one syllable,
yet no less significant for that.
It could have slipped through my fingers
or fallen from my heart,
escaping unnoticed
while I was out of my depth in the chaos of life.

I searched everywhere,
on top of the wardrobe,
down the back of the sofa,
in the bottom of the deepest drawer,
tipped out and picked through black sacks of emotions.
Cautiously lifting the corner of the relationship carpet
I discovered it there,
duplicated
in bold and italics, capitals and lowercase,
dust-covered and forlorn,
embracing the names of discarded lovers,
now only used for cute dogs and expensive shoes.
My tongue presses against the roof of my mouth,
forming the word,
oh, so nearly saying it …

Closing my eyes, I'm fifteen again,
in the back of a Mini, in a quiet dark lane,
my mouth is full of someone else's tongue
and the lost word tastes far sweeter than it sounds.

After the Storm

Rain came in horizontal sheets,
boiling the surface of the sea
and slubbing windows.
Lightening fractured the sky.
I paced, pocket full of secrets,
my plans on hold,
until I could bear it no longer.
Slipping out of the house unnoticed,
shoes in hand, rucksack over shoulder,
striding out towards La Rouge Terrier,
right at The Barracks,
past deserted silver mines,
their chimneys crumbling,
to the headland,
sparse tufts of grass
clinging to the rock.

Waiting for the tide to ebb,
ribbons of magma appear
within the amphibolite mass
with each backwash.
Cautious descent,
grazed knees, stubbed toes,
inhospitable terrain,
subterranean caves:
'a Fat Man's Misery'.

I scratched your name on skim stones
bouncing them into oblivion
and when you didn't appear
I smoked a cigarette very slowly
then buried my sorrow beneath
a tuft of sea grass
and dived into
The Venus Pool.

Other Publications by Dempsey & Windle in 2017

Collections

Loving by Will by Timothy Adès (second ed.)
ISBN 978-1-907435-40-9
£7.99

*

Part of the Dark by Scott Elder
ISBN:978-1-907435-45-4
£7.99

*

And No Birds Sing by Kyle McHale
ISBN 978-1-907435-42-3
£6.99

*

Gerry Sweeney's Mammy by Dónall Dempsey
ISBN: 978-1-907435-47-8
£7.99

•

Bridges by Gary Allen
ISBN: 978-1-907435-51-5
£7.99

*

Anthology

Poems to Keep edited by Janice Dempsey
ISBN 978-1-907435-43-0
£8.99

*

Pamphlets

A Talent for Hats by Fiona Sinclair
ISBN 978-1-907435-39-3
£6.99
*

A History Nailed Down by Ray Pool
ISBN 978-1-907435-41-6
£6.99
*

Sprouts by Alexandra Davis
ISBN: 978-1-907435-46-1
£6.00
*

Shall Have to Stop Now by Wanda Barford
ISBN: 978-1-907435-44-7
£6.99
*

Owl Lit by Ian Clarke
ISBN: 978-1907435-52-2
£6.99

******

All are available to order at dempseyandwindle.co.uk,
amazon.co.uk
and through bookshops.